Eight Questions About Sexuality

by

John Patterson

Grosvenor House
Publishing Limited

The right of John Patterson to be identified as the author of this
work has been asserted in accordance with Section 78
of the Copyright, Designs and Patents Act 1988

The book cover is copyright to John Patterson

This book is published by
Grosvenor House Publishing Ltd
Link House
140 The Broadway, Tolworth, Surrey, KT6 7HT.
www.grosvenorhousepublishing.co.uk

A CIP record for this book
is available from the British Library

ISBN 978-1-83975-156-1

TABLE OF CONTENTS

Bible quotations are taken from the New
International Version.

Preface

Human sexuality is a hot topic in society today. In recent years the debate has become more heated, more wide ranging and more polarised. Furthermore, opinion in society as a whole, and in some cases the law of the land, have also changed out of all recognition compared to where they were only a few years ago.

I have tried to marshal some of the comments and questions that frequently crop up in the debate about sexuality, and I have tried to give some answers from the Christian point of view as I understand it.

I have included an introductory section called "Why is the Bible Important?" Here I have tried to explain the central place that the Bible has in a Christian's beliefs and behaviour. Reading this passage will, I hope, help to explain some of the answers I give to the questions I ask.

ACKNOWLEDGEMENTS

Several people read through this document when it was in draft form and I want to thank John Kirkland, John Chester, Jackie Appleby and John Dawson for their comments. The document changed considerably as a result of their input. That said, they do not necessarily endorse what remains. For that I am wholly responsible.

WHY IS THE BIBLE IMPORTANT?

Christians believe that God has spoken to his world. They also believe that he still speaks to his world. One of the ways that he does this is through the Bible, sometimes also called the Scriptures.

Many people in recent years have explored the Christian faith through the Alpha course. In the book that underpins the course, Nicky Gumbel says this about the Bible:

> Paul [an early Christian leader] wrote of the inspiration of the Scriptures that were available to him: "All scripture is God-breathed and is useful for teaching, rebuking, correcting and training in righteousness, so that God's servant may be thoroughly equipped for every good work." (2 Timothy 3:16-17).
>
> The Greek word for "God-breathed" is *theopneustos*. It is often translated as "inspired by God"; but literally it means "God-breathed". The writer is saying that Scripture is God speaking. Of course he used human authors. The Bible was written over a period of 1,500 years by at least forty authors from a wide variety of backgrounds – kings, scholars, philosophers, fishermen, poets, statesmen, historians and doctors. The Bible is 100 per cent the work of human beings but it is also 100 per cent inspired by God (just as Jesus is fully human and fully God).[1]

---

[1] Gumbel, N., *Questions of Life*, 2nd ed, Alpha International (2010) pp. 82–83

This is important because for Christians, the teaching of the Bible is the God-given guide to what we believe and to how we behave. In any discussion on any moral topic, the Christian's first response will be, "What does the Bible say about that?"

Someone may object, "How on earth can you be serious about a book that is already some 2,000 years old, and some of it much older?" In what other area of life would you turn to something as old as that for advice?" Another objection might be, "Who says that the Bible is the word of God? What's the authority behind that claim?"

If the Bible is one way in which God speaks to us, the coming of Jesus Christ to this earth is another, and is indeed the supreme way. This is how one of the Bible writers puts it:

> "In the past God spoke to our forefathers through the prophets at many times and in various ways, but in these last days he has spoken to us by his Son, whom he appointed heir of all things, and through whom he made the universe. The Son is the radiance of God's glory and the exact representation of his being, sustaining all things by his powerful word. After he had provided purification for sins, he sat down at the right hand of the Majesty in heaven."[2]

Humanly speaking, Jesus was born into a family in Palestine about 2,000 years ago. But events around the time of his birth, and then the way his life unfolded, left some convinced that Jesus was more than a human being.

---

[2] Hebrews 1: 1-3

Even at the age of 12 he showed an awareness of being God's son and, in conversation with the religious teachers of the time, astonished all who heard him by his understanding and his answers.[3] When he left the carpenter's shop and became a preacher instead, people hung on his words. He could speak about God with an authority which even the religious leaders did not have.[4] Miracles were common around Jesus. He healed the sick, calmed a storm, raised the dead to life and much, much more. In his hands a boy's small picnic became a meal for thousands. So it continued for three years, and gradually the impression grew among some that God was in their midst.

All of this came to a shuddering halt one Friday. Following a long period of hostility towards him by some religious leaders who were jealous of his powers, Jesus had been arrested the evening before and the judge, despite believing that Jesus was innocent, caved in to the hostile crowd and handed him over for execution. By the Friday afternoon it was all over. Jesus was dead. So they buried him in a tomb and sealed it.

Two days later a strange rumour started to circulate. First of all, the tomb was empty but the wrappings around Jesus' body were exactly where they would have been if the body had still been there. Then one, and another and another became convinced that they had seen Jesus alive in a new way and that he had actually spoken to them. Gradually the conviction grew and spread that God had raised Jesus from death to life and that Jesus was now alive. Then his followers remembered

---

[3] Luke 2: 41–52
[4] Matthew 7: 28–29

that Jesus had told them when he was with them that this would happen, but at the time it just did not register what he was talking about.

Over the next six weeks the risen Jesus appeared and reappeared to his followers, and more than 500 people became convinced that he really was alive. Jesus also spent time giving instructions to his inner circle and teaching them further about the kingdom of God. Shortly before leaving them to rejoin his Father in heaven, he told them to wait in Jerusalem till they were given the power they needed to be God's witnesses worldwide. Their commission was to "go and make disciples of all nations, baptizing them ... and teaching them to obey everything I have commanded you."[5]

Ten days later God's power fell on the waiting believers in the person of the Holy Spirit. Convinced that the moment had come, they began to share their faith. The worldwide spread of Jesus's message was under way and has continued to the present day. It is also part of Christian belief that at some point in the future, a point that God will determine, Jesus will return to judge all people of every nation and generation, and then a new era in God's plan will begin.

It is central to the belief of the Christian church that Jesus was and is the Son of God. A carpenter and preacher, yes, but fully God as well as fully man.

This brings us back to a question asked earlier in this section, "Who says that the Bible is the word of God?" The short answer to that is that Jesus, the Son of God,

---

[5] Matthew 28: 19–20

says that the Bible is the word of God. That needs some further explanation.

If you open a Bible it is divided into two sections. The first part is called the Old Testament. This part contains the holy writings of the Jews and, as he grew up, Jesus would have heard these read in the synagogue week by week. This was the record of what God had done for his people and what he had said to them down the centuries until the time of Jesus. For them this was the word of God.

That was also Jesus's view of these writings. He studied the Old Testament carefully and shaped his life and teaching in accordance with it. He regarded it as inspired by God and as authoritative both for himself and for others.[6]

The New Testament, the second part of the Bible, did not then exist, but Jesus made provision for its writing. Out of the many people who followed him Jesus chose a particular group of 12 people to be his inner circle. He called them "apostles"[7]. The word conveys the idea of being "official representatives". They had particularly close contact with Jesus from the start of his work in public and all except Judas Iscariot were witnesses to the resurrection of Jesus from the dead. (By then Judas was dead.) As well as the ability to perform miracles, Jesus assured them that the Holy Spirit of God would give them special help in recalling his words and in deepening their understanding when he was no longer with them.[8]

---

[6] E.M.B. Green, *The Authority of Scripture*, Falcon Booklets (1963) pp.11–17

[7] A few were added later such as Matthias, Paul, James the Lord's brother, and perhaps one or two others. See footnote 9 below.

[8] John 14: 25–26; John 16: 12–15.

It seems reasonable to infer from these arrangements that Jesus was, among other things, putting in place the group of people who would compile the authoritative record of his life, death, resurrection and ascension into heaven and of all that flowed from those events. Their record would also be the authoritative record of the teaching of Jesus. This is how the early Christians saw it because when, in the fourth century after Jesus, the church came finally to settle which writings should be in the New Testament and which not, the test was whether a particular writing had come from the hand of an apostle, or, if it hadn't, had it at least come from someone close to the apostolic circle and have apostolic authority behind it.[9]

To sum up, Christians regard the Bible as the word of God because of the authority of Jesus Christ. He, the Son of God, regarded the Old Testament as the word of God. He, the Son of God, laid the foundation for the writing of the New Testament. Can this book have any greater authority behind it? This matters, because in the questions that follow my aim will be to show how I believe that the Bible answers those questions. Our own opinions are simply that – our own opinions. They can be formed by those close to us, by society in general, by our own make-up and by our own preferences. But if God has spoken on a particular matter, then that is to be the Christian's guide both for what we believe and for how we behave.

The question may then be asked, whether, as Christians, we are meant to follow every word of the Bible exactly as it was written, and the answer to that is no. The Old Testament charts the journey of God's people over

---

[9] J.R.W. Stott, *Understanding the Bible*. Scripture Union (2003) Chapter 6

centuries, and in that time God was gradually teaching them about himself. But the practice of sacrificing animals to pay for sin, for example, which we find in the Old Testament and which helped people to understand the seriousness of sin, was made redundant once Jesus Christ died on the cross. Once that had happened animal sacrifice had no further purpose. So the ceremonial law of the Old Testament was set aside, but what about the moral law?

There are Christians who believe that the Bible should have no back cover on it. In other words, Jesus has set the ball rolling but it is up to each new generation to work things out as seems best to them, and not be tied to the teaching of the past. For example, some who argue in favour of homosexual activity will say that our psychological insights today are so much more up to date and advanced that we cannot possibly be limited by teaching which is 2,000 years old. They will also say that, whereas casual promiscuous sex may be ruled out, that is quite different from sexual activity within a stable, loving and faithful relationship.

Someone has framed the question like this:

> How can a divine revelation given in transient cultural terms have permanent validity? How can a revelation addressed to a particular cultural situation have a universal application? Does not the cultural conditioning of Scripture limit its relevance to us, and even its authority over us?[10]

---

[10] J.R.W. Stott, *The Contemporary Christian*, InterVarsity Press (1995) p.194

John Stott, who asks that question, goes on to answer it along the following lines. All of us have several sets of clothes, such as our work clothes, our party clothes, our doing-dirty-jobs clothes and our night clothes. But, regardless of which set of clothes I am wearing at any one time, the person underneath does not change, and my character and personality remain the same. So it is with God. God revealed his will to the writers of the Bible over a period of some 1,500 years and in many different cultures. Jesus himself was born into a particular culture at a particular time. What matters is not the culture (the clothes), but what God has said, commanded, forbidden and promised.

For example, in John chapter 13, we read how Jesus, on the night before his death, washed the feet of his disciples, a job commonly done in Palestine by a slave. Such an action made perfect sense at the time because roads were dusty and guests arriving at a house needed to freshen up. Nowadays, however, willingness to do the menial tasks would take a different form, like being willing to bag up the rubbish for the binmen, or clean up the mess the cat has made on the carpet. The setting (the clothes) has changed, but the willingness to do the unpleasant tasks has not.

God's nature does not change, and as Christians we are not free to depart from what God in Scripture teaches, forbids, promises or commands. In the New Testament Jesus consistently upholds God's moral law. "Anyone who breaks one of the least of these commandments and teaches others to do the same will be called least in the kingdom of heaven, but whoever practises and teaches these commands will be called great in the kingdom of heaven."[11] So, far from setting aside God's moral law, Jesus deepens and extends it. For example, when speaking about adultery, he makes it clear that it is not just the act of adultery that is wrong, but the lustful thought behind the act.[12]

So in trying to solve any moral problem the Christian's guiding principle will be to ask what God's word says about it. And when Christians try to set forth what the Bible teaches on any issue, they aspire to set forth not their own opinions but what they believe that God says through his word.

---

[11] Matthew 5: 19
[12] Matthew 5: 27–28

Some Terms and Definitions

Every subject has its own terms and shorthand, and sexuality is no different. In trying to offer some terms and definitions I have drawn material from a number of sources such as Wikipedia, the NHS, the BBC and various internet sources, though the final form of words is my own.

Male is sometimes represented by the symbol

Female is sometimes represented by the symbol

Heterosexual/straight
Heterosexuality is romantic attraction, sexual attraction or sexual behaviour between persons of the opposite sex or gender.

Homosexual/gay/queer
Homosexuality is romantic attraction, sexual attraction or sexual behaviour between members of the same sex or gender. As a sexual orientation, homosexuality is a continuing pattern of emotional, romantic, and/or sexual attraction to people of the same sex. It is an interesting turn of the wheel that "queer", which 50 years ago was a somewhat insulting term, is not now necessarily so.

Lesbian
A lesbian is a homosexual woman who is sexually attracted to other women.

EIGHT QUESTIONS ABOUT SEXUALITY

1. Why does the church make such a fuss about sex?

Sexual intercourse between a man and a woman who are married is one of God's gifts to mankind. It is, of course, how human beings keep reproducing but it is also meant, within the setting of heterosexual marriage, to be a physical means of cementing an emotional bond.

Sex is a powerful drive but, like every other part of us, has been affected by mankind's disobedience to God. It is part of our fallen nature and, if allowed to run out of control, can be a source of harm.

A coal fire burning in a grate is safe. It gives light, warmth and comfort to those who stand near it. But if the fire falls out of the grate and onto the carpet, it can be a threat to life itself.

Similarly God has put sexual relations within heterosexual marriage.[14] If this boundary is respected, that is the "grate" in which this good gift can be safely used. If it falls out of the grate, people can be hurt. When adultery takes place, both families may suffer lasting damage, and it is often the innocent who suffer as well as the guilty. Children, in particular, may suffer through the break-up of their families.

---

[14] Genesis 2: 24; Matthew 19: 3–6; Ephesians 5: 31–32

So how we use sex matters. A view is sometimes expressed that rules take away our freedom. The fact is, however, that without some rules life does not work. Think of driving in a world where no one had to stop at traffic lights unless they wanted to, and where no motorist had to give way to any other. Think of a game of tennis in which no one had to play within the lines on a court, or in which a player having trouble with his serve could simply lower the net. The game becomes meaningless and breaks down. The rules of driving and tennis, and much else besides, give us the freedom and framework within which these activities are possible.

This is no less true of God's rules about sex, and if we feel that God's rules are restrictive it is worth remembering that he created us and loves us, and that his rules are for the good of ourselves and of other people.

This issue also matters because it raises the question of whether we are serious about the Bible's teaching being the word of God. If we can ignore the Bible's teaching about sexual behaviour, why should we feel bound by anything else it says?

2. What about deep same-sex friendships?

Whereas many will find companionship and fulfilment in marriage, many will also remain single. The latter may not have the opportunity to marry because they don't meet the right person. Or they may have no appetite for marriage but still need company and support. Or their marriage may have ended through death or the breakdown of a marriage. Or they may have denied themselves marriage for the sake of God's work. Whatever the reason, God has said, "It is not good for the man [or the woman, we may add] to be alone. I will make a helper suitable for him [or her]".[15]

The single state is seen as a high calling in the Bible,[16] but single people need the support of friends and others if they are to flourish. The people of God are meant to be one source of such support. To call someone a brother in Christ or a sister in Christ is not only a spiritual reality but implies new privileges and responsibilities. For some, fellow Christians may be a more real family in terms of love and support than any blood relations they may have, and there is nothing wrong at all with deep friendships between people of the same sex.

---

[15] Genesis 2: 18
[16] 1 Corinthians 7

One of the strongest same-sex friendships in the Bible is that between Jonathan, a son of King Saul, and David. "After David had finished talking with Saul, Jonathan became one in spirit with David, and he loved him as himself. ... And Jonathan made a covenant with David because he loved him as himself."[17] Jonathan was as good as his word and helped David in different ways, even though that exposed him to the anger of his father.[18] When it became clear that Saul meant to kill David as well as Jonathan, and Jonathan and David needed to part, their parting showed the depth of their relationship. "Then they kissed each other and wept together–but David wept the most. Jonathan said to David, 'Go in peace, for we have sworn friendship with each other in the name of the Lord'..."[19] The Bible has no problem at all with deep same-sex friendships.

[17] 1 Samuel 18: 1, 3
[18] 1 Samuel 20: 30–34
[19] 1 Samuel 20: 41–42

3. Is it wrong to have sexual thoughts about other people?

Touch is a basic way in which human beings express emotion. Babies and children thrive on hugs and cuddles and kisses. This is how family members show love and acceptance. As we grow up, there is a natural desire to touch and be touched by those we find attractive. But part of growing up is also about learning that some kinds of touch are appropriate and some aren't. Hugging a family member may be fine, but hugging a stranger may bring danger. And we also learn what kind of touch is appropriate. Shaking hands will offend no one, but touching someone in an intimate area of their body will cause offence. The teenage years bring extra challenges. As our bodies mature sexually there may be an increasing desire to express our feelings in a sexual way. These feelings may be towards people of our own sex or of the opposite sex, and having crushes on people at this stage is just part of life. As we grow up, we have to navigate this sea of feelings and attractions and learn to chart a course through it.

When it comes to trying to sort out what is right and wrong in these matters, Christians make a distinction between orientation and action. Orientation is about whether we are sexually attracted to people of the same sex (homosexual), to people of both sexes (bisexual) or to people of the opposite sex (heterosexual). There has been much discussion about what causes us to lean in one direction or another. Some say it is to do with our genes (nature), some say it is to do with our upbringing (nurture) and some say both. Whatever is the right answer to that question, there is no condemnation in our orientation, any more than we can be fairly blamed for having curly hair or blue eyes. It seems to me a matter of regret that some Christians have suffered agonies just for feeling same-sex attraction. When it comes to our actions, however, the Bible is clear.

The second chapter of Genesis gives a lengthy description of how God creates woman as a partner suitable for man. Near the end of the chapter come the words, "For this reason a man will leave his father and mother and be united to his wife, and they will become one flesh."[20]

These are important words. Jesus, when arguing with some of the religious leaders about divorce [21], repeats them and the apostle Paul, when likening marriage to the relationship between Jesus Christ and the church, also uses them.[22]

One aspect of this relationship is its permanence ("be united to" is literally "sticks to"). A second is that the man's first loyalty is no longer to his parents but to his wife ("leave his father and mother and be united to his wife"). God's fifth commandment[23] to his people will remind them of their perpetual duty to honour their fathers and mothers, but there is no conflict with what is said here. The man and the woman are a new family unit whose primary loyalty under God is now to each other. And the fact that there is a new family unit means that marriage has a public aspect as well as a personal one. In addition, the marriage is exclusive of

---

[20] Genesis 2: 24
[21] Matthew 19: 5–6
[22] Ephesians 5: 31–32
[23] Exodus 20: 12

all others. No second husband is provided for the woman and no second wife is provided for the man. Although polygamy (a man having more than one wife) is recorded in the Old Testament, the norm in Scripture comes to be that "marriage is an exclusive heterosexual covenant between one man and one woman, ordained and sealed by God, preceded by a public leaving of parents, consummated in sexual union, issuing in a permanent mutually supportive partnership, and normally crowned with the gift of children."[24] Any sexual relationships outside this bond are explicitly forbidden, for example fornication[25], adultery[26], homosexual genital acts[27] and sex with animals (bestiality)[28].

We cannot help our orientation (how we are attracted) but we can help how we behave (our actions). This is a crucial distinction and failure to make it bedevils much discussion about sexuality. A further point here is that, even if we are tempted to stray outside the boundaries that God has given us, temptation itself is not the same as sin, and some have suffered agonies just because they have been tempted. But Jesus himself was tempted.[29] Martin Luther, the pioneer of the Reformation, once said about this distinction between temptation and sin, "You cannot keep birds from flying over your head, but you can keep them from building a nest in your hair." And, of course, if we do sin, God offers forgiveness to believers because Jesus has already paid the price for our sins on the cross.

---

[24] Stott, J., *Issues Facing Christians Today*, Inter-Varsity Press 2nd ed. (1990) p.289
[25] Acts 15: 20
[26] Exodus 20: 14
[27] Romans 1: 26–27
[28] Leviticus 18: 23
[29] Luke 4: 1–12

4. Why, according to the Bible, should straight people be allowed to have sex but not gay people?

The setting in which God has placed sex involves a man and a woman who are married. So, according to the Bible's teaching, the single straight person is not at liberty to sleep around. The married couple whose sexual relationship has broken down are not at liberty to seek sex outside their marriage. The divorced person is not at liberty to have sex unless he or she remarries. The widow or widower is not at liberty to have sex unless he or she remarries. Thus, a sexual relationship is, according to the Bible's teaching, off limits for many people; it is not only gay people who are called upon to do without sex. And we need to keep reminding ourselves that the God who made these rules designed and created us, knows us better than we know ourselves and wants us and others to flourish.

5. Why should straight people have a choice about marriage, but, according to the Bible's teaching, not gay people?

The first problem is that sex has become an obsession in our society. There is almost the feeling that life without sex is an incomplete life. That is not the Bible's view. While it does assume that heterosexual marriage will be the norm for most people,[30] that does not imply that everyone should be married or that life without sex is some kind of second-rate life. Jesus makes it clear that the richest experience that life has to offer comes from our being connected to him[31], not to whether we are having sex or not. Many in religious orders have lived lives of fulfilment and achievement, and yet the renouncing of marriage (and therefore of sex) will be one of the vows that they have taken in choosing their way of life. And, of course, such achievement and fulfilment have been experienced by many single people who are not in religious orders. It does not mean that, if sex is forbidden to us, there won't be frustration, and even failure, in trying to live God's way. But it does mean that sexual activity is not essential to life as God has designed it.

A second reason why gay genital relationships are forbidden by the Bible is because they reverse God's

---

[30] 1 Corinthians 7: 2
[31] John 10: 10

order of things. In Romans chapter 1 the apostle Paul attempts to paint the big picture. He has never visited the Christians of Rome but he hopes to do so. In his letter to them he sets out his understanding of why the human race finds itself in the mess it is in. This analysis applies to you, to me and to every human being without exception. It is an ugly picture. Here's a taste of what the Bible says:

> For although they [human beings] knew God, they neither glorified him as God nor gave thanks to him, but their thinking became futile and their foolish hearts were darkened. Although they claimed to be wise, they became fools and exchanged the glory of the immortal God for images made to look like a mortal human being and birds and animals and reptiles.[32]

The man and the woman disobeyed God at the time of creation and the fall of mankind from God's grace has comprehensively disordered our lives as human beings. The passage quoted above is saying the same thing. Our failure to honour God as God, together with ingratitude and futile thinking, is just part of the mess. In believing that we are wise, we are actually fools. Instead of worshipping God as he is, we make an image of him and worship that instead. The rebellion of the human race against God's way of living has sent us into reverse.

The passage above has the words, "They became fools and exchanged the glory of the immortal God for images made to look like a mortal human being and birds and animals and reptiles." I want to dwell for a moment on the word "exchanged".[33] This implies a swap. I let go of

---

[32] Romans 1: 21–23
[33] Romans 1: 23

one thing and I take something else instead. As the apostle Paul goes on to develop this theme, he will use the word twice more.

> Therefore God gave them [us] over in the sinful desires of their [our] hearts to sexual impurity for the degrading of their [our] bodies with one another. They [we] exchanged the truth of God for a lie, and worshipped and served created things rather than the Creator – who is for ever praised. Amen.[34]

I have inserted the words "we", "us" and "our" in square brackets to show that the Bible's diagnosis of what is wrong with human beings ("they") is actually about every single one of us. The passage is describing a universal problem, but in the end it boils down to you and me. This time, when Paul uses the word "exchanged"[35] he says that we have exchanged "the truth of God for a lie". We have let go the truth and grasped a lie. Is it possible for us to make any greater error than that?

The passage continues:

> Because of this, God gave them over to shameful lusts. Even their women exchanged natural relations for unnatural ones. In the same way the men also abandoned natural relations with women and were inflamed with lust for one another. Men committed indecent acts with other men, and received in themselves the due penalty for their perversion.[36]

---

[34] Romans 1: 24–25
[35] Romans 1: 25
[36] Romans 1: 26–27

The word "exchanged" appears again, for the third time in four verses.[37] Paul wrote in Greek and on the first occasion he has used a straightforward form of the verb "exchanged". When he uses it for the second and third time, he uses a stronger form of the verb, as if saying "they have completely exchanged". It seems to me that he is making the point that homosexual genital acts embody physically the way we have, in our fallen state, reversed God's plan for creation. So, far from gay marriage being a legitimate extension of heterosexual marriage, it is, if we take the words of Romans seriously, a reversal of God's intention for sexual activity.

If we think that God's wrath is directed only, or mainly, at homosexual genital acts, we need to read on:

> Furthermore, since they [we] did not think it worth while to retain the knowledge of God, he gave them [us] over to a depraved mind, to do what ought not to be done. They [we] have become filled with every kind of wickedness, evil, greed and depravity. They [we] are full of envy, murder, strife, deceit and malice. They [we] are gossips, slanderers, God-haters, insolent, arrogant and boastful; they [we] invent ways of doing evil; they [we] disobey their [our] parents; they [we] are senseless, faithless, heartless, ruthless.[38]

We may protest that we do not fall into all these categories. But can we say that we are not guilty of any of them, at least to some degree? Paul's purpose in this first chapter of Romans is to portray how black and bleak the human condition without God is, and this includes our sexuality.

---

[37] Romans 1: 26
[38] Romans 1: 28–31

He does this, however, in order to prepare us, later in the letter, for how God has made it possible for us to be rescued from this situation.

A final word before we leave this passage in Romans. There is an argument around today which goes something like this: "What Paul is condemning here is casual sex between people of the same sex. But that is quite different from a sexual relationship between two gay people who are in a long-term loving, faithful relationship. Therefore this passage can be discounted." I personally believe that there is no support in the passage for making that distinction. The opening chapter of Romans is one of the most global statements that Paul makes about how sin has ravaged mankind (all of us). While love and faithfulness are good qualities in any relationship, I can see nothing here to indicate that Paul is only talking about casual sex. And even if this passage is set aside, what about other Bible passages in which same-sex genital acts are described as wrong?[39]

---

[39] 1 Corinthians 6, 9: 1 Timothy 1: 10

6. The law of the land allows gay marriage. Why doesn't the church fall in line?

What I have said already shows that what the state now allows concerning gay marriage is in direct conflict with what the Bible teaches about heterosexual marriage. There is now pressure on the church, from outside and from some inside, to change its position also. Some would say that the church is failing to move with the times. The government's emphasis on equality and diversity has increased the pressure on the church.

As has been said earlier, the disobedience of the man and the woman at the time of creation means that we are alienated from God. Our rebellion has sent us in the opposite direction from the one he intended us to go in. When God enables us to turn around (repentance), to accept his forgiveness and start a new journey with Him, he begins to remake us.

Sometimes people will say, "Surely God accepts me as I am" and they mean by that that they do not have to change their behaviour. But this is a misunderstanding. It is true that God accepts all of us exactly as we are but transformation of our characters is God's agenda from the word go. The apostle Paul puts it like this, "We ... are being transformed into his likeness [the likeness of Jesus] with ever increasing glory, which comes from the Lord who is the Spirit."[40]

Furthermore, it's not a solo effort; we do it together with other Christians (the church). This community, living now for God rather than against Him, will seek to live as he wants and to march to his beat. So there is now a contrast, even a conflict, between the way the church wants to live and the way the world wants to live.

The Bible speaks about this often. Writing to the Christians at Rome Paul says, "Do not conform any longer to the pattern of this world, but be transformed by the renewing of your mind. Then you will be able to test and approve what God's will is – his good, pleasing and perfect will."[41]

Sometimes the law of the land runs parallel to what the Bible teaches, and sometimes it does not. For example, the Bible teaches that we may not steal, and the state agrees. But sometimes the law of the land is silent when the Bible clearly speaks. In the Bible, committing adultery (a married person having sex outside marriage) is a sin. But a person who is known to have committed adultery will not be taken to court in the UK because adultery, however much it may be frowned on, is not against the law of the land.

I use that example simply to show that sometimes God's law and human law agree; sometimes God's law will speak when human law is silent, and sometimes God's law and human law will be in direct conflict. It is the

---

[40] 2 Corinthians 3: 18
[41] Romans 12: 2

church's job not to take its cue from what society is doing, but rather to live in God's way even if that is unpopular and against the grain of society around us.

At a time when Christian faith was central to this country's life, it is not surprising that Christian principles greatly influenced the laws that were made. As our nation has, to a large degree, moved away from Christian faith, so some of our laws have done the same. This means that Christians wanting to be faithful to the Bible's teaching will sometimes be uneasy with laws that are being passed. They may find themselves in direct disagreement, or even conflict, with them.

7. What is homophobia?

The opening paragraph of Wikipedia's article on homophobia says this:

"**Homophobia** encompasses a range of negative attitudes and feelings toward homosexuality or people who are identified or perceived as being lesbian, gay, bisexual or transgender (LGBT). It has been defined as contempt, prejudice, aversion, hatred or antipathy, may be based on irrational fear, and is often related to religious beliefs."

(I have not included references to source material given in the paragraph above, but these can be found in the original Wikipedia article.)

If we express disagreement with homosexual genital acts we are likely to encounter some stiff opposition, and before long we are likely to be labelled "homophobic".

While it is true that some who disagree with homosexual activity may feel irrational hostility towards gay people, and thus deserve the homophobic label, that by no means speaks for everybody. The Wikipedia definition doesn't seem to allow for the fact that many Christians oppose homosexual activity for reasons that have nothing to do with contempt, prejudice, aversion, hatred, antipathy or irrational fear. The Wikipedia definition comes close to implying that religious belief is the source of these negative attitudes. In some cases it may be, but it does not do justice to the fact that many Christians who oppose homosexual activity do so because they believe that God's word says it is wrong. And they do so with charity and humility. Christians who find themselves accused of homophobia should, of course, check that their attitudes to gay people are above reproach, but they have every right to express a considered opinion on this as on any other moral question. Indeed we must go further.

If, as Christians, we believe that homosexual genital activity is wrong because God says it is wrong, how can we not speak out? In what sense can we be said to have other people's welfare at heart if we let them continue unchallenged in activity which we believe is against God's will, and therefore against their own and other people's good? I would not oppose homosexual genital activity myself if it were just down to me, but I cannot read the consistent teaching of Scripture and say it is all right. And it is not just heterosexual people saying it. There are gay Christians who, in obedience to the teaching of the Bible, say the same thing. Groups such as Living Out[42] and True Freedom Trust[43] witness to the costly stand of some of these gay believers.

One last comment on homophobia. Often this word is weaponised to intimidate and silence those who believe that homosexual genital acts are wrong. It works like this. The person whose behaviour is being challenged resents the fact of being challenged. So, rather than engaging with the challenge in a rational and charitable way, he or she labels the opponent homophobic, as if to say, "There is something wrong with you, the challenger, rather than

---

[42] www.livingout.org
[43] www.truefreedomtrust.co.uk

with me who is being challenged." This puts the challenger on the back foot, especially if they fear that some kind of hate crime may be alleged, and the conversation may go no further. As I have said above, we must strive to ensure that our own attitudes are above reproach, and we must do all in our power to treat others with respect and gentleness. But we must not be bullied or intimidated into silence. As Christians we have an obligation to hold up God's pattern for human flourishing, and that will mean persevering in making the case for a biblical understanding of sexual relationships.

8. What is transgender about?

In the Bible's account of creation, we read the following: "So God created man in his own image, in the image of God he created him; male and female he created them."[44]

From time immemorial the understanding of most people has been that there are two sexes or genders, namely male and female. If at birth a baby's genitals are male, the baby will be considered a boy. If the genitals are female, the baby will be considered a girl. (In a tiny number of cases the baby's genitals may not be clearly those of a male or those of a female (intersex)).

There are a few people, however, who feel that they are in the "wrong" body. So somebody who, biologically speaking, is male may think of himself as female. And somebody who is, biologically speaking, female may think of herself as male.

These feelings of being in the wrong body may go back to early years. My understanding is that those who experience them do not do so out of any conscious choice, and often find coping with such feelings a prolonged and distressing experience. "Gender dysphoria" is the term often given to people wrestling with this feeling of being in the wrong body.

For some people, this identification with the opposite gender is so strong that their overriding desire is to

---

[44] Genesis 1: 27

change (or "transition") to the opposite sex. This transitioning process may be assisted by surgery or drugs, but the outcome will be a "trans" or "transgender" man or woman. A transgender man is biologically female but now identifies as a man. A transgender woman is biologically male but now identifies as a woman.

What are we to make of this? Before we explore this further, it is well to remind ourselves that, for the people concerned, this is a painful situation:

> We need to begin by remembering that we are not simply talking about "issues" here, but people: precious individuals, each created and loved by God. Most of them don't have a strong political agenda or any desire to fight in a "culture war"; they are simply trying to cope with feelings that may well cause them great distress. Too often they are being damaged in the crossfire of what can become a very heated debate. ... I do think Christians should contribute to that public discussion, but it is vitally important that we do so with great sensitivity and compassion.[45]

Other family members may well be drawn into the pain of this situation.

When it comes to the issue of what lies behind transgenderism, there are, broadly speaking, two different understandings of what is going on, and therefore two different views about how we should proceed.

One school of thought believes that feelings are all-important. If you feel that you have become trapped in the wrong body (and some people feel it very strongly), your

---

[45] Roberts, V., *Transgender*, The Good Book Company (2016).

feelings should be your guide. You should have every encouragement to be the "real" you, and your position should be protected by the law of the land. In the UK the Gender Recognition Act of 2004 charts the way that a trans person can move legally from one gender to another, and, as I write, the government has recently finished consulting on whether this should be made easier than it is at the moment.

The second school of thought resists this approach. It believes that the feeling of being in the wrong body is the result of psychological conflicts within the person concerned. An example of this is a child we will call Andy.

Between the ages of three and five Andy increasingly started playing with girls' toys and with girls and began saying that he was a girl.

He and his parents were referred for family therapy. During one session Andy said that his parents did not love him as a boy, so the way to get their love was to be a girl. What had led to Andy's conclusion? When he was three his sister was born, but she had special needs and needed significant extra care and attention. Andy had concluded, wrongly, that being a girl was the way to be loved by his parents. Family therapy helped Andy and his parents to identify this misunderstanding and to straighten things out. But some today would argue that Andy really was a girl and was in the wrong body.[46]

Dr Paul McHugh, for some 40 years Professor of Psychiatry at the Johns Hopkins Medical School in the USA, writes as follows:

---

[46] Dr. Michelle Cretella, *The Daily Signal,* speaking in a video called "Pediatrician Shuts Down Leftists on Puberty Blockers", 24 May, 2018.

https://www.facebook.com/TheDailySignalNews/videos/8394 25636265031/

"At Johns Hopkins, after pioneering sex-change surgery, we demonstrated that the practice brought no important benefits. As a result, we stopped offering that form of treatment in the 1970s."

He continues, "First, though, let us address the basic assumption ... the idea that exchange of one's sex is possible. It, like the storied Emperor, is starkly, nakedly false. Transgendered men do not become women, nor do transgendered women become men. All ... become feminized men or masculinized women, counterfeits or impersonators of the sex with which they 'identify'. In that lies their problematic future."[47]

It would be hard to find a greater chasm between the two sides of this debate, but finding the right way ahead matters greatly. If we wrongly encourage children and young people who have transgender feelings to believe that they are in the wrong body and that drugs and surgery are sometimes the way to change this, we are sentencing them to years of potentially harmful treatment, with no certain resolution of their conflict at the end of it. Indeed, some evidence seems to point in the opposite direction as Dr McHugh describes:

> The most thorough follow-up of sex-reassigned people – extending over thirty years and conducted in Sweden, where the country is strongly supportive of the transgendered – documents their lifelong mental unrest. Ten to fifteen years after surgical reassignment, the suicide rate of those who had

---

[47] McHugh, P., 'Transgenderism: A Pathogenic Meme', *Public Discourse*, 10 June 2015. ©The Witherspoon Institute

undergone sex-reassignment surgery rose to twenty times that of comparable peers.[48]

I have already stressed our need to follow the word of God in making sense of God's world, and that is no different here. God has created the human race in his own image and has created us male and female.

Dr Michelle Cretella, President of the American College of Paediatricians, comments:

> Our bodies declare our sex. Biological sex is not assigned. Sex is determined at conception by our DNA, stamped into every cell of our bodies. Human sexuality is binary. Either you have a normal Y chromosome and develop into a male, or you don't and you will develop into a female. There are at least 6,500 genetic differences between men and women. Hormones and surgery cannot and do not change this.

Dr Cretella continues:

> To indoctrinate all children from preschool forward with the lie that they could be trapped in the wrong body disrupts the very foundation of a child's reality testing. If a child can't trust the reality of their physical bodies, who or what can they trust? Transgender ideology in schools is psychological abuse that often leads to chemical castration, sterilization and surgical mutilation. If that's not child abuse … what is?[49]

---

[48] As above

[49] Dr. Michelle Cretella ,*The Daily Signal*, speaking in a video called "Pediatrician Shuts Down Leftists on Puberty Blockers", 24 May, 2018.
https://www.facebook.com/TheDailySignalNews/videos/8394 25636265031/

Dr Cretella's views are hotly disputed by some other clinicians, but her comments are a measure of the widely polarised views on this subject.

What might be the reason that this desire to change genders is so strong in some people? Despite God's original creation being perfect, the fall of mankind in Genesis chapter 3 had catastrophic consequences for all of us. Every part of us – mind, body, spirit and emotions – has suffered and does not now function as God had intended. It should not be surprising that gender and sexuality have been caught up in this process. Add in all the misconceptions that children can collect as they grow up, as with Andy above, and you have a rich source of possible confusion. The Bible tells us that God created the human race male and female. The current departure from this truth is sowing a world of confusion, and children and young people, and their families, are the ones who are likely to be hurt.

And finally...

In less than 20 years, what is legally possible in relationships in the UK has changed dramatically. In 2004 the Gender Recognition Act allowed people with gender dysphoria to change their legal gender. In the same year the Civil Partnerships Act gave a same-sex couple rights and responsibilities similar to those of a man and a woman who were married. In the recent past this legislation has been extended to heterosexual couples who want some legal protections for their relationship but who do not want to be married. In 2013, and a year later in Scotland, the Marriage (Same Sex Couples) Act was passed, and same sex marriage is now allowed in Northern Ireland. The twin claims of equality and diversity, admirable in some respects but misleading in others, have helped the process along. By any standard this is an avalanche of social change and, like any avalanche, we have yet to see where it will end up and what will happen along the way.

As much that is central to Christian teaching is swept away by these changes, standing in front of the avalanche can feel like a lonely place to be. And yet, as Christians, we are called to be salt and light in a nation that has largely turned its back on Christian teaching. Scripture warns that bucking the trend is precisely what we sometimes have to do to live in God's way.[50] If the Bible's teaching alone will truly promote a right understanding of human beings and

---

[50] Romans 12: 2

42

of God's purposes for human relationships, now more than ever that voice needs to be heard.

Tackling these issues is not an end in itself. Our behaviour matters because it has spiritual implications both for time and for eternity. When Paul writes to the Christians in Galatia he contrasts the kind of life that will result when we follow our own human inclinations with the kind of life that will result when we follow God's Holy Spirit. Having listed a string of sins in the former category, some of which are sexual and some not, Paul says, "I warn you, as I did before, that those who live like this will not inherit the kingdom of God."[51] He is sounding both a moral and a spiritual health warning which we ignore at our peril.

It can sound both tolerant and loving to go with the flow and let people do whatever they want to do. God, however, speaking through the pages of the Bible, tells us something different. Knowing that as human beings we have lost our way, he recalls us to his way and makes that journey possible for those who will respond. Furthermore, he tells us that seeking to live in his way and to proclaim his way will bring us grief (as well as joy) this side of heaven.[52] But still we are told to do it. True love dares to say hard things because turning a blind eye to behaviour that God forbids puts the eternal safety of ourselves and others at risk. And we make no presumption to speak on our own authority. We say what we believe that God says in the pages of Scripture. Human flourishing is God's plan for his world, and it comes on his terms, not ours.

February 2020

---

[51] Galatians 5: 16–25
[52] Matthew 5: 11–12